GREYLIGHT

This is dedicated to all those who have
supported my writing and life the last 20 years.

Cecilie E Roaldset
GREYLIGHT

Editing and layout by Greg Dent
Cover and interior art by Cecilie E Roaldset

Epidemic Books
Seattle

GREYLIGHT

Copyright © 2018 by Cecilie E Roaldset
Poems written between 2003 and 2018
All rights reserved

An Epidemic Book
Published by Epidemic Books, Co. Ltd.
Seattle, WA

www.epidemicbooks.com

ISBN 978-1-949058-00-0
Printed in the United States of America

FOREWARD

I have been a writer since the early 1990's when I performed my first open mic in the high school talent show. This collection of poems is from the last 20 years, and covers a wide scope of topics. I find my inspiration in people and the greylight before the sun comes up.

If you like my work and would like to follow me on a regular basis you're welcome to check out my WordPress blog: cecilieroaldset.com, where I write about my daily struggles and my future goals.

In the age of pictures and Instagram it's more important to me that the words I write carry weight, not just pretty pictures.

I would like to thank all those who have stood by me in the last two decades and those who have given me inspiration. My canvas is words that tell a story, I hope you enjoy mine.

Best,
   - Cecilie E Roaldset

PUSHING PUSHING

Have you seen me in the corner
Pushing, pushing.
I can feel the warmth of his body,
sound of his voice
unfaltering on my life of broken glass.

Pushing, pushing.
Intimacy and stability scares me;
as a woman counting flaws
comparing myself to corporate whore
magazines with air-brushed beauty.

Pushing, pushing.
I count me—
I count I,
the woman
that won't introduce you to what
some people call family.

I count myself—
watching redness from crying in the mirror
watching smiling families—
hearing stories about childhoods,
fairy tales; to mine—
emotional mind bombs and blurred lines.

Pushing, pushing.

Waking up with you beside me.

Still
I wonder,
maybe I
question too much—
to want me—
a tomboy that climbed trees,
that took karate not ballet.

Pushing, pushing.

That stood alone when everyone
had someone to hold
someone to fight with.

Pushing, pushing—
Hold me when my emotional seas throw me.
Hold me when the doubt creeps in,
that one day you will have become another story.

CER 2004-2018

ELLIS ISLAND

Journey began nearly 10. Welcome!

To east-coast fast-paced coke-induced hysteria,
demarcation was my accent, heavy on tongue—Lead.
Leaving valley of yellow wheat in Summer, decorated by lush
Winter snowfall, sound of cross-country skis.

Our neighborhood was cold, shivers ran down my spine—as no one
greeted the renters, new yet secondhand in the mouth of Reagan.

Cars and huge vans our enemy, as children stepped off curbs
into arms of strange men, later to become faces on milk cartons.
Silence broken by racing sirens chasing accidents on the Merritt
Parkway, gliding by, heading straight for the mouth of The Apple,
chasing Vermont's leaves. My father educated me on sirens,
as if their wails would somehow prevent the unknown.

Strangeness of large aisles, eating 1980's junk food out of boxes,
market cereal. Tony the Tiger had already been introduced at my
grandfather's house tucked between Stockholm and Norway.
My mother held onto home in wheat bread my sister and I would
consume while still hot, stomachaches erupting.
Angry at toast, lashing out over our Americana, she would yell.

Eating savory slices not enough, eating liver with diligence of immigrant prowess.

Trained monkey repeating simple phrases, insulting with sweetness of voice, being asked from where I came was homework. Explained.

My first kiss thought I had come hazel-eyed from South America, missing my homeland by half the globe.

Hair graced my shoulders, two summers of one-hundred degrees shedding my immigrant self in locks. Conformity becoming survival the way mountain climbers only carry what they need, losing my country through sounds of words.
It became homework, learning how to lose my heritage as it sat on my tongue, arching itself into sentences.

I am an immigrant,
who saw the Statue of Liberty and climbed
the elevator of tower two.
Eating strange-tasting cheese,
Decorating sandwiches with cod eggs.
I am one part this and one part that.
Shaken and stirred, blended yet full.

Watching a suitcase shredded by immigration at JFK,
tears filled my father's eyes as he swore in all the tongues he
knew in one breath. Air India, decorated saris and beautiful colors,
watching open-mouthed suitcases as they danced around a
crowded conveyer belt.

History placed quotas on mankind, one part Asian,
one part European, three parts English, bowing to Hoover.
Remembering a conversation, lopsided, blinded by the slums
of Brooklyn, Bronx, Lower Eastside—plain Americana.
BUT: Didn't your grandparents sail on a small boat
slaughtered by waves, holding onto your dreams.
Reply filled with hatred, as if less than her Irish roots,
decorating her eyes and hair four generations later.

Holding onto sound of mother tongue dancing in conversations,
oblique and hidden by proper English.
Holding onto sound of cross-country skis and large fir
trees heavy with snow—taste of Winter in a cup.
Holding onto my heritage in food, music
and footballs kicked not thrown across green grass.

CER 2004-2017

SUN SLANTS

Sun slants through small, open windows and sticky air; colored houses pass me slowly—families, smiling kids—and summer sneaks in between the slants in the windows, drifting by mountains, clouds that sit watching hikers.

When space fills between slanted windows, I watch rust on lamp posts—outdated, ancient lightbulbs; red brick buildings, gargoyles; trees that shade the past as it dances between generations.

Spent love fills my lungs with oxygen as I race with myself, watching what is gone—what was never mine—in grey light of morning. Curves the color of olives and eyes the color of seaweed; love becomes a marathon.

Tall masts, long winding stairs; mud fills space on the steps, mud fills my soul—like soot it sits as I fight the past. Morphing into a punching bag to suit my betrayers; seeing their deceit line my street for an afternoon parade.

I was too naive, wanting too much, my grandfather's words fall like lead-based paint, poisoning my resolve. Screams echoed at my mother; smells of fresh-baked bread decorated fights.

Up north between slits of midsummer sun, my hero grandfather ravaged wine, choking down camels. Corner of the living room, space filled with his shadow where weather became king.

Lust comes in early-morning grey light—slender frame, curly hair—and then slips out; fences greener. I watch almost love, almost lust, as he steps backward rather than forward, caught in contradictions.

Sun slants through glasses and eyes the color of seaweed, leaves that decorate east-coast fall. Wandering, plugs in my ears, I miss sirens, fighting couples, and hurled insults.

I remember rust and chips, surrounded by wooden bowls and love's first kiss, nerves bouncing from wall to closets. I chase love, sitting fog hanging necklaces around northern mountains.

Sails drift out of slips into evening light, bonfire where lust dances as the flames grew; piles of receipts. Trust slips back in, hiding in the corner. I watch the world drifting through the slants in the windows.

CER 2005-2017

WHITE PICKET FENCES

Erecting white picket fences, mowed lawns,
prestige of
looking good leaves wholesomeness dropped
to the ground; thick dust of
flakes—empty men with pockets full.

Well-dressed men with bad intentions, abortion vacation,
trapped within 4 walls with hollowed men. I lost my virginity
to misplaced trust, locked dorm doors,
sharp edges of a mirror, rough hands, sodomy.

My body became a barely functioning machine,
knees wobbling and bruised limbs—lost in
grey light, childhood of the adult he stole. Smell of
salt, acrid smell of cum.

I stopped feeling,
breathing, tucked between my chest cavity.
Virginity was thrown up against a sink, in a town
where white picket fences and trophies hid bruises.
Someday soon you will know who has survived.

CER 2005-2018

5:45 AM

Five forty five AM,
her voice knocks
on the Tricks
that show in her
Eyes when she speaks.

Her friend is coming
to drive her to Arizona at
eight Thirty Sharp.

Look at how dirty the
sidewalk is she says
comparing it to Phoenix
where they are Clean.

Someone stole her life in
20 minutes over a locker.
Between the inches
Between I found

Rest.

Graylight wake-up calls
cloudy with doubt. Shadows,
light came in soft sheets and showers.

I began believing. Every night was
one sheet.

Warmth of hot showers, thrill of
holding a key,
space, every thing
glides between five-forty
five am.

Simple
a new start, leaving coffee-stained
floors, roll call and shadows of
summer-homeless, balancing medication
for something grander

than my name misspelled
small tight shrugs-cold mats,
hope that came through
in the dark clouds.

Her eyes change
when she speaks.
Can you hear her Now
Knocking.

CER 2007-2018

GOLDEN OAK

My first love sound
baritone of cello,
vibrating strings a soft case,
cheap three-quarter size.

Wrapped by legs carrying it
proudly when I could barely
form sentences in English.
Playing scales, small notes on a page.

My ear learned to listen to violins,
screeching through their notes.
Playing principal chair the first time.

Conductor cuing me
hands sweeping in curve,
bringing in second violins and finally
we stopped.

Silence, swept over us—
threatening wave of whispers.
Turning slowly toward
Violins, his hands stopped plainly

right in front... her.

She acted innocent—starting a
fight with our conductor.
Blaming—The Cellos.

Missing her cue, sitting quietly,
conductor telling her
to count; lecturing her on,
leading the first violins.

Rehearsals getting longer,
growing into golden oak, a
full-size smell of carpet in the
music store, I had my own room.

Scales, bows—hours passed,
I settled on a beautiful full-
size golden oak.
Imported from Germany.

Mature age of 13—speaking my first
English sentences leaving the store.
My accent still heavy.
I had a weapon—a cello.

I switched teachers, Suzuki, traditional,

meeting Yo Yo Ma after a concert.
Making chocolate milk—
bribing myself playing 45 minutes
6 days a week.

Playing quartets, playing second chair
Pachabal's Canon, slow moving sludge.
Silent auctions, chamber of commerce
providing music.

Door to door—selling Indian River Oranges,
new strings—trips to nationals in Virginia.
Long bus rides, long rehearsals—
Placed first Virginia Beach.

High school—I driving my Mother's
Buick Le Mans, plastic interior, chasing
last bell greeted with singing of Cecilia.

Blushing ear to ear finding my seat,
principals playing West Side Story,
beat-beat-voice, beat, beat, beat, voice,
drinking gallons of Coca Cola.

Production running till 11PM we moved
rehearsals up, bringing dinner, eating
junk food, chasing exhaustion. We Made It!

Sitting twelve in the pit—breathing, smiling,
Cast parties, hugs, people attending college,
Leaving; The Met. Our small,
unrehearsed orchestra played

Alice Tully Hall at The Met.
Opened, harshly out of sync
Filled with jitters we went humbly
back to our seats, defeated by ourselves,
Pressure.

Sitting high above audience in awe.
The world famous British orchestra
was on a world tour.

Parents always telling us we did Great,
Really Great—when our end pins fell.
Our strings became too hot under light,
missing cues.

Some of my friends would smile nodding,
claiming discourse, We Sucked Mom. Heads
down—we left our whites and blacks,
tucked out in demonstration.

Dripping sweat down our faces, cool cases,

Gloves in winter, cold hands, strings are
harder to warm, Golden Oak back in case.

Senior year of high school,
Humanities debates ensued,
long, arguing. Taking out paint,
I said my peace.

Imagination doesn't always have to have meaning
White paint on a blue case. Silently taking my seat
in class—traveling fast.

Lady Grey climbing behind me, tucking
behind the back of the chair, practicing
drawn the sound purring
in contentment when I practiced.

Breaking strings, re-stringing my bow,
Golden Oak sitting in my room, comfort,
Wrapped my legs around its wood.
I know each mark.

It's my child, my first love,
Sound forever trapped, eight years
of baritone, aching arms, scales and concerts.

CER 2003-2018

SLIPPED LOVERS

Slipped lovers glide
through my dreams:
Botticelli paintings, Greek
sculptures of mistaken lust
runs through fingers. Grey
light chases mornings, shadow
smoke, bars, aftershave, curves of
backs, arms, hands, lover
that swung right.

Lust would take silhouettes of love,
glinting evening sun. Fumbling words,
tip of tongue,
promises,
hands glide into jeans, shirts,
boxers, left reminders, tip tongue
moments, scent of sex
lingered in a 2 story walk-up.

Questions—maybes or could've
beens. Mary jane induced fights,
scent of skin clung to sheets,
condom wrappers became confetti—
exploration of touch, orgasms came,

first small tokens, soreness draped,
my body making it light.

Haunted by curly hair, infatuation
chased us that summer; the way
animals chase prey. Circling
each other, drawn to flames;
a definitive night left me
scarred, mistaken trust,
turned to anger. Lust turned
to bitterness coming with fall;
one leaf, nor'easter, he
tore from my heart.

My first love arrived, mustang,
tools decorated my life; idealistic
dreams concocted out of mary jane,
waking me in grey light coming back from
work.

Red hair wrapped my heart in heat of a cold
summer, watching from a distance wondering,
he still holds on as I steady
myself and the boat that has been
my life.

Blond hair came unexpected, held on
while walking away. Infused wood-sap-
stained jeans, sweetness. Loss came
folding in heat, summer of change.

Glimpsing faces of could've
beens, flashes of lust, come
in small waves. I have not made a choice
in a boat of life called love.

CER 2004-2017

SINGLE PLY

The toilet paper is single ply,
feeling cheap in an expensive bathroom.

I watch as he pulls out his gallon of cheap whiskey
every night after the bottle of wine that must
accompany dinner.

Clinking of ice cubes, watering down
what has already been watered down.
He has a place for his whiskey glass,
a coaster that stays put
among the books.

I miss my single shot of Caol Ila
and wonder at the single ply toilet paper
and the crumbless counter tops.

Walking 8 miles a day is my escape;
from the knives and the cheap whiskey—
90 minutes of beats.

I breathe—the stale New England air,
missing mountains, wagging tails,
and my husband's warm hands.

CER 2017

PERFECT HALVES

I.
Shells, spiky, broken in perfect halves, lying strewn,
treasure-filled with smooth, round brown.
Grade-school teachers, competition between small pockets
in coats collecting
Fall.

Falling blustery wind echoes leaves swaying, sounds of rain,
between laptops & school boxes, clustered ipods,cell phone
conversations. I find
deeply entrenched eyes, stoic stares—
love
sits on the tip of my tongue,
neither walking away from it—nor
expecting, I close the book.

II.
Lightswitches always sit on the left wall
inside hospital bathrooms.
Fidgeting & uncomfortable, watching how
her rave lipstick matches
her shirt.
Between now & later he shows up, mapping out conversation,
certainly I am not sure.

Somewhere between Cointreau-laced chocolate,
600 miles of travel, smiles
greet me.
I no longer hold my breath, expect great things
from meek people.

Fall's cold reaches, its arm stretching into my bedroom,
tucked between sheets
dreams float to the surface.
Speed—high school hallways treating sleep as illness
that will rob them of titles & scholarships.
Click-heavy doors that unlock when handle turns,
click clockwise,
NBA players.
Ultrasounds—measuring my pelvis. Lightswitches
sitting on the left,
click of a switch, room lighting.

III.
Cold hands on laptops, no one speaks whole sentences.
Whispered insults
slip through. I wonder if I am chasing love?
Nightmares catching me in
my sleep.

Balancing act between where I was/am,
remembering tight small beds,
false promises, threats dancing from tongue.
Seeds of pomegranates,
how far I have come, lost in false embraces,
attempting to let him in by
spoonfuls.
I won't allow myself to feel.

Leaves blowing in waves close to the ground, crunching
feeling Winter
in northern gusts, spitting rain.

IV.
Sitting engulfed in comfy chairs surrounded by ipods,
headphones, watching my
neighbor clean his lawn, blocking out sounds & life.
Children's laughter, sirens,
orange creeping hollows eve.
Tired of counting lovers, slipped through fingers, hearing
stories of nieces
collecting 200 chestnuts, shades of foundation covering
dark circles
disappointment,
shame,
guilt.

My old self in their eyes, feet surrounded by ice & glass.
Convictions
of happiness framed by parenthesis.
Friendship extends a hand through
muddled fog & loss of direction.

V.
Turning on the light, counting steps, spaces in-between.
Mud filled paths, freedom tucked between fog & mountains,
rain sits, heavy drops on delicate fruit.
Wind plows north, dark clouds, balance
brightness before rain.

CER 2005-2017

YOGA MASTER

I.
Candlelight bounces
tracing
between calf muscles,
dipping into jeans.
Downbeats bounce
within a square
room.
Breathe
pain & release
pain to release.
Candlelight shields early
morning weekend
sunlight.
Stop.
Counting tequila shots,
concentrating on
happiness.
Running into old friends,
between downbeats
candlelight illuminates the
shadows
between future & past.

II.
Wrapped stocking chairs,
sawdust, windchimed boxes.
Figure
split between
man\woman\woman\man
reminiscent of
middlesex,
division of pink versus blue,
gentrification.
Sadness over completion,
bubblegum tables,
alchemy,
number 7 doors.
Literal pain, sitting
below
toilet bowls.
Sound of paper blowing
in the wind.
Hindu icons move
removeable heads.
Heat of the sun;
parched souls seeking
comfort in chocolate-
covered espresso.

III.
Worlds collide,
drip coffee & espresso;
latte versus
drip,
Dunkin' Donuts
versus Hines.
Pink kite extends
on arm,
reaching
to gusts bouncing
off mountains,
swirling
feelings left in
songs of David Gray,
putting to rest Adam & Eve.
Yankees
versus
Red Sox.
Sound of paper
echoes,
leaves, planes approaching,
engines,
choir
music bounces; tea
candles, embrace & chance.

Candlelight bounces between
shadows past, present,
sliced on walls.

CER 2017

LIFE STANDS

I.
Four inches 2 feet tall, my life stands
tarnished, scraped & bumped.

Long distance accusations—
hope becomes lost in chaos, choices &
mistakes too late to pick up and put back together.

Four inches 2 feet tall, my life stands, reminding me
of how trust is frail. Lies & ivory towers dismantle ideas
of what I thought love was.

Now gathering chestnuts; cold hands in pockets.
Fall rolls into Winter, sudden stretched-out mass. I
stand looking at love—a word hollow to the tongue,
escaping, alluding butterflies, cocoon.

II.
Sun shifts in the horizon, my mind balances reaction
& emotion, truth & lies. Babies carved
out of mother's turmoil.
We tuck between pillows, lies beneath us.

Rugs we use to show hurt—open, swinging, perpetual motion.
Underneath it all we are naked on soul's branch.

III.
Seeing love, once he sat inches away. Hearing my cello as orchestra becomes hikes. In your eyes permanently tucked between Say Anything & senior prom. He told I couldn't see trees for forests.

IV.
Outlines of mountains seen on maps, wrapped in fog,
Sul doc, haunting. Outlines, sketches—ovals left open,
broken hearts exposed.
I glue hope with a needle & thread,
stitching hope & reality with
abstract wantonness. Balanced my left & right brain,
counting car alarms, chaos.

Propagated seedless love scrapes on my life as it stands
2 feet 4 inches.
Tomorrow extends outward, balancing outlines of mountains,
hope stitched into canvas of cells, arms wrapped.

CER 2002 - 2017

SAFETY-GOGGLED LIFE

Between the masts, wired fences, I can make out mountains
in greyish blue—penciled out on the horizon.
I can feel my pulse, smell the village I grew up in,
looking at birch trees' small leaves swaying
in the wind. I can hear my grandmother in her kitchen,
smell of sugar-

pans filling her small counters,
cousins still come digging for worms, bait
fishing far north in the tundra.
Pounding headache, planes orbit dumping fuel,
bracing for the worst. I shut the TV off, grab a book & run.

Laparoscopic incision below belly button,
echoes with hammers, nails
hitting particle board, soon to be home.
She's never alone, grasping onto
lovers; she marries/divorces, calling love a favor,
a piece of gum.

Her lovers swallow her identity—she goes from
wearing color to
morbid boyfriend & one word replies.
Art, love, disjointed conversation
cut & pasted together.
Wondering what she fears—if being alone is harmful.

Writing poetry, I can hardly hear the difference
between where she begins
& her lover starts—passing judgements, meant to strike,
increasing her average, leveraging insults.
Between time & bus stops, I count lost,
missing & addictions, banners
in the distance. I see confusion before it shows up.
I find hearts in my lattes, smiles with my coffee.

Crushes that pass—I miss acrid-smelling cities of my youth,
recall cold hurting my lungs, crisp
morning, empty rural streets. Sheep grazing next to a
thousand-year-old church. Embracing silence, my body tires
quickly, no longer looking for another rest stop.

No longer living fear. Sitting in crowded coffee shops, I drown
in chaos of other people's lives as they swing through the doors,
apprehension clearly written in their expressions.
Small prayers & doubt, smiles, children's cold feet.

Leaving my anger one hot summer day, I saw lost love;
knowing forgiveness was no longer
hard to master.

CER 2006-2018

SLOW TANGO

Wonder-lust crawls through veins,
Pure.
No amount of running will make my filled
heart forget skin's shadow in early morning
grey light.

Te amo

His dark eyes twinkling, hearing
sonnets' song, Douglas Coupland's
words whispered in touches of fingertips

reminding me of New York City, hard-edged
boys forming shells in code, later spelled
out in glimpses of words.

Jeg elsker deg

Tracing each tattoo as it spreads with wings
across his arms, tucked between one bone
and the next, lines becoming curves to

shyness announced in smiles.
Sitting within reach of my breath, eyes
peaking, catching glimpses.

Te amo

Tucked into my existence between layers
of life—sonnets of experience. William Blake
coating lungs, industrial revolutions,
esprit de corps.

Whispered in circumstances becoming a game,
wonder-lust, slow tango moves in three-four time,
one sweep left, two sweeps right.

Jeg elsker deg

Legs become entangled, steps change
direction, sweeps come as moments' breath
captured by lenses of life.

His dark voice on lines of paper, consigning
myself to wonder-lust, each moment wondering
if sonnets of Shakespeare dance within his laughter.

CER 2004-2017

OHANA

Hawai'ian for never leaving anyone behind.

My mother watching anger curling my father's voice,
laced with snaking threats.

Claws of hands clasped around
throat, temporarily floating,

hovering above parquet floor.
Airwaves contracting, twisting,

my neck.
Blackness encompassing sight.

Mother stood—
not fighting for my life.

Until, terminal seconds passed.
She, prying his hands off me,

collapsing to the floor, barely able
to focus, trying to

call for help, animals chasing
room to room,

until I managed to lock a door.
Frightening breaths dialed known

digits. Watching trees fade,
waiting till sirens came.

My mother left me behind that day.
My mother belittles,

Spitting insults, rain pellets
covering my soul—

slime that I no longer feel
as she left me,

as my neck twisted,
leaving trust forever behind.

Appearances, functions, my other sister
have all but replaced.

What she has grown tired of—
blame; antagonizing, she

circles a predator to prey, first wider
circles and smaller, and smaller.

Speaking to me in the same voice she did when
I was a child.

Big words leave her mouth—
decency, respect, tide of blame—

sludge. Low tide, she presses my buttons,
wondering at

eruptions as she stands telling,
justifying her abuse.

Claim grows wider, as she can't be responsible, for eruptions
as her perfect story unravels, and rain pellets
my soul—

as she does what she knows best,
blame the child she never really

wanted.

CER 2003-2018

LOVE AS PUNCTUATION

Love is punctuation
without grammar; a
long drawn-out sentence
I lost faith in.

Punctured by stabs—
neighbors fighting;
married with doses of anger,
door slamming.

Love is old couples
that have survived
knowing bliss is a consequence,
not a chess piece.

Punctuated with slow-moving tides,
altered times.
I watch them holding hands,
talking in whispers,
gestures my lovers
never mastered.

I saw just married on a car last year,
two happy people staggering slowly
towards middle age.

Punctured by the idea of fault
he drifted away—
loss settles on my soul,
filament that won't scrape off.

Realizing love is a not a contract,
a four-letter word; it glides with
humility in a wind of faith.
Taken away by riptides on
moment's notice.

It's a love poem about ants and rocks,
summer storms, round bellies,
now is tarnished, rusted bike
gathering spider webs.

Love is Not,
Just do it
a fuck,
a one night stand,
loneliness lurking in dark corners,
love can't fit on a page of ink,
love is lost in a photograph.

Love is grammar without punctuation,
Adulation without admiration,
Scribble left on bathroom walls,
Late night phone calls,
Hope tucked away.

CER 2017

SINGLE

To all the men I have never slept with:
I see you in corners, over cheap beer, pool tables. Huddled
and plotting, laughter sneaks across your face,
turning, catching my eye.

Maybe it's your eyes, mouth, body—short,
tall, medium, waif. Hair that hasn't seen a barber since....
Color of sand, coal, straw, curly, straight, mohawks, streaked
blond, gel towers.

Sunburn, shades of white, fine olive oil, dark chocolate,
muscles shown, hidden in tight t-shirts, button-downs,
turtlenecks, sweaters.

Hard firmness wakes as you catch my smile—gazing
your sex hardens, blushing, temptation hidden in
Carhartts, khakis, tight jeans you have worn on purpose.

I wonder what your kisses feel like—how you look
in morning as sun graces your eyes, muscles hidden
beneath clothes.

I stare at you in awe—
As you take my breath away without speaking,
hands clasping mine, tension in your back.
Infatuation rises, a flood,

calming as I see the redness of cheap beer in your eyes,
reeking of cologne, gel, aftershave, beer, and a performance
I don't want to see—

even in the front row.

CER 2017

WORDS CURL

I.
Words curl into his mouth; a haystack with needle and lies
become a game. Twisting my heart into shapes and tossing
away self-esteem.

My body curls into his in early morning, grey light
sweeping into the room—our world of chaos, our
manufactured wars.

Turmoil we choose to make, wars we choose to start.
Trust. A fragile, papier-mâché newborn baby; it has to
be built.

To some, trust is a joke at the end of a movie. To have faith
in love used to be a grand piano, silver keys of ivory;
its notes clean and clear—

becoming muddled, distorted, out of sync.
Swallowing emotions—they run towards my left shoulder;
pinched nerve, migraines

I can feel days before they happen, coming in waves of
fatigue, spreading through my blood, lowering my voice.
The pain sits on a perch on my left shoulder, reminding me
of how heavy emotions run—trapping itself in my left shoulder.

Lovers drifting by on street corners, watching as their shadows
extend out and away; headlights bring frames forward.
Retracting and expanding, watching the shadows of lost
lovers drifting closer rather than far—focal points,
a map of my past.

II.
Broken spine of my futon, I left next to a dumpster,
pine split in two—one piece my past; one my future.
Humidity of east-coast Summers

floated up to my apartment, wondering if the ink
would melt off the page of Lady Chatterley's Lover. I sit
listening to plight of college, textbooks, choices; Summers
where work was a hobby and the future was far away.

Eating at a table by himself, his posture
and eyes speak louder than the words forming in
his mind. He was a chestnut ripened too late,

curled into my pocket. My first apartment sat perched next
to a highway extending north. Neighborhood crawled with
bar fights on the weekend, arguments over parking spaces,
sirens screeched down the street 5 days a week.

Wails of gunshots, fires and chaos; hot bagels in paper bags;
humidity dancing on the sidewalk; Yalies versus Townies;
age-old arguments balancing his life between two poles—
each step more confident. Sometimes

love becomes icing, frosting, confetti scattered in the wind;
clear lines become blurred, obscuring truth. Lens cutting through
the fog—love was golden, princes riding horses,
fairy tale endings, cleaning away poor self-esteem with a mop.
Solving the shattered-glass lies, come in the shape of a pen,
a pink dress, and being seen as beautiful now as I gather withered
vines of lies, wrapped closely in the box of my past.

I don't look, because the love I saw was never real.
It was silken sheets of lies, kisses. What was true
gathering in the aftermath of the storm that was once love.
I don't look back to the fog in his eyes.

CER 2004-2018

SNUGGLED WITH TIME

Listening, I can hear stories that only expressions show;
small feet dance in Fall's school dance.
Seeing parents, lined up waiting
for yellow plowing down streets.
Between dirty steps and dog leashes I find my heart
open, breathing in Fall's cold air.

Between time I find space—solid-quiet.
My body remembers cramped quarters,
native dances, fear in the eyes of strangers;
searching for sleep—hard to find.
Distance expands; my heart heals slowly,
patching up cracks left raw, open.

The acrid smell of New York City seeping
into my hair, clothes. Memories dance;
I cross bridges. Hellos turn into hour-long
conversations without introduction.
Train glides north, away from cityscapes;
suits and shopping bags sit side by side.

I crawl into my past, small town—placed on sound and river.
Watching super-stretched
limos, white wedding gowns. Noxious celebrities
sway with breeze. Time becomes a
rubber band; my heart hurts saying goodbye
to what was anchored 3000 miles away.

Tucked between mountain ranges, avalanches,
and bitter cold; finding small pockets
in your clothes to enter.
Lovers that still find space between the past and present.
I see shadows and feel emptiness in my bed—
long shadows, disbelief a badge

I wear. My soul feels like marmalade, bitter yet sweet.
Counting excuses, lines
I have heard before—watching
as my past sails by on empty streets. Listening, I can
hear stories that only expressions show,
small feet dance in Fall's school dance.

CER 2005-2018

HEART REQUIRES PRECISION

Dissection requires instruments,
a heart is fragile,
a supple mass that must be sliced with precision.

Pay no attention to emotionally charged statements
that fall from tattered lips. Slice heart
in four ways—creating the most damage to victim of
lust or love. dc sleeps, pacing, between tissues and a pipe.

Blue smoke reaches an arm forward, pulling ideas,
floating above pieces of a broken heart.
Dissection requires instruments, a heart is a fragile
supple mass that must be sliced with precision.

Pay no attention to love extended into limos and rented tuxes,
making commitment by duct tape,
connecting the bumper falling off of love to cars.
Tuning belt spinning and squeals; slashed hearts
tattered, splashed across the internet and bathroom stalls.

A heart is fragile, supple mass,
tying together the old and fragile, bound by their walkers,
shadows of bombs, striped coffins and death.
Chasing dreams stuffed behind dusty corners and lies.
A heart

tucked between ribs in chest.
dc sleeps alone tonight catching moon
on his bright PJs. A heart starts beating
slowly.

CER 2004-2018

HOLLOW

I.
Hands slide across my body
tracing each curve;
my body becomes a destination
point, map. Hands fall into crevices,
across my breasts; lips dance down
to hollowness of my neck, tucked between time.

Morning becomes slow hot afternoon as his
body heats, peeling covers, hands gliding across
my body, creating a new destination. I leave my old
cold lover behind. Warmth of sheets, a new day.

II.
Chasing memories, burning incense and loss.
Remembering Fall's emptiness. Red leaves hold
Spring's sun, swaying in the afternoon light.
Consequence.
Taking out a new map,
tracing each step

as I leave behind my old self in Fall, heat on futons,
morning sun. Expectation—a word too heavy for my new
heart—placing it in the corner as each step taken floods
each crevice with doubt.

III.
Hands gliding down my body leave me feeling empty,
love left through the back door I can no longer
leave ajar. Stepping forward, feeling energy of the past
draping each vein in my back, moving slowly, seeing
shadows of other hands, other mornings,
sugar coated promises. Left my heart stinging.
Green eyes chase me from one lover to the next,
shaking past memories in my jar.

IV.
Feeling the map that is my body, waking
to empty, fresh sheets—grinding my past lovers to
finite dust. Stretching each curve of my body, his hands
that leave me in wonderment.

Hollowness of my neck,
density of thought, stacking lovers lost to
morning's bright sun. Feeling my old self,
tucked between Spring Street and Canal.

I step out of my futon balanced by bricks,
looking towards mountains, inhaling a sweet
lover's scent, Dragon on his arm, drifting into
afternoon's sun.

CER 2004-2018

I AM

The girl that got away,
The long goodnight kiss,
The rape survivor.

The feminist,
The tomboy,
The strategist,
Patience,
Solace,
Deep thinker.

The debater,
The motivator,
The silhouette,
The sunshine,
The wind blowing through
The trees.

The realist,
The final goodbye,
The ex-girlfriend,
The hand holding yours,
The soft lips in
The morning.

The luster,
The lusted,
The object,
The subject,
The narrative.

The hugger,
The sweetie,
The one
You know,
The skier,
The biker,
The risk taker.

The fisher,
The catcher,
The cutie,
The one you think is innocent,
The crossed,
The blessed,
The straight talker.

The tipper,
The Dutch date,
The screw,

The morning after,
The nooner,
The editor,
The writer,
The poet.

The one holding your hand,
The one that will believe,
The one that never falters,
The riptide,
The Nor'Easter,
The hurricane.

The plot,
The screenplay,
The truth teller,
The sympathy,
The empathy,
The faith.

Hazel eyes,
The traditionalist,
The theorist,
The art lover,
The anger,
The calm.

The sweaty palm,

The cello player,

The skirt wearer,

The east coaster,

The grande latte drinker.

The cheesecake lover,

The one missing bagels,

The hiker,

The camper.

Desedemona,

The purveyor of truth,

The consequence,

The bitch,

The lame-o,

The missing,

The mediator,

Eye of

The storm,

The wish,

The parted,

The coming,

A woman.

CER 2003-2018

TRACK 22

Mouth opens to sky filled with zodiac; flashbulbs from cameras.
Impatience stands by the information booth, waiting.

Announcements over the PA—blinking train tracks & men in
fatigues greet me. Street opens to car horns & midweek,
midtown mayhem.

Sitting @ Rockefeller center counting tour books & cameras.
Greeted by loss & joy, Saint Patrick's opens its arms wide,

pulling me in. Listening to languages,
cameras coming in for solitude & pain.
Sitting front row—listening to echoes of souls bouncing off

the stained windows, leaping across marble floors.
Tree-line means
I'm @ the park—crowds thinning & doormen appear,
flagging taxis; ordered cars, where Money is.

Crossing

across eastside, old Irish bars that survived, stand firmly
through temporary cosmopolitans, fusion menus.

Watching

my old self, I find solitude over a plate of waffles & intimacy
of weddings
3000 miles away from home.

Downtown

heading towards Lexington—suits having lunch—daily grind.
Down into the 6; waiting minutes, while smelling stale air,
rats scurry, tucked between time out & college students
I go downtown, walking
familiar corners; I find indecision in a dressing room.
Whistling to Blur—we change.

Wondering what is exactly
behind door number two, three. Late summer heat brings
hormones to the surfaces like small flames. On a street

corner

fate stands lost & indecisive, time is only something that catches us
@ Grand Central—venus' flytrap. Pondering stroll & watching
landmarks pass,

seeing myself twenty years earlier;

tired feet finds track 22, leaving zodiacs,

20-second crushes, smell of acid air, yellow cabs,

125th street station

announces my departure.

CER 2005-2018

Cecilie E Roaldset is a writer/poet and double immigrant who has written since the early 1990's. She currently lives in Bergen, Norway with her husband and their dog. Cecilie is inspired by nature, people and current events. You can often find her reading about current affairs and fiction. She enjoys hiking and being outside.

Her poems are written to be read out loud, and most of them in this collection were crafted for the Seattle open mic scene in the early 2000s.

www.ingramcontent.com/pod-product-compliance
Lightning Source LLC
Chambersburg PA
CBHW041803160426
43191CB00001B/22